Paul W

The Greatest Business Quotes

Inspirational Quotes

That Will Change Your Life

Introduction

Business is all about an opportunity, a plan, efficient management and execution, and of course marketing. This is true for businesses of all sizes – from large corporations with a worldwide presence, to small mom-and-pop home initiatives. And yet, there's something, without which, no business can succeed. That is inspiration and motivation.

Every business owner, manager, and even the employees must remain motivated or inspired to succeed. Business is often a long-drawn process. You have to keep doing the same things over and over again for several years. There can, and often will be distractions. Not all days will be the same. In fact, some days could be so bad that you might want to quit altogether and do something else. That's where motivation and inspiration can help. It can help you maintain focus, give you a vision of the larger picture, remind you of where you want to be, so that you keep doing what you are best at.

Successful people are all motivated individuals. They all have this common characteristic about them. But they too have their individual low-moments, when things are not going according to plan. However, they manage to stick around and overcome their difficulties in the end. That's what makes the critical difference.

You can learn from what they do. Many successful business people will read books and biographies of others who have stood out. Others read inspirational quotes to keep them going.

Yes, inspirational quotes can certainly help. These are thoughts and ideas of people who have achieved a lot in life and business. These quotes tell you what they are thinking, and how they want to achieve amazing results.

You can gain too from inspirational quotes. So here are some of the finest inspirational quotes from proven achievers in life and business – people we all look up to often for inspiration.

"Time is the friend of the wonderful business, the enemy of the mediocre."

— Warren Buffett

"The problem is never how to get new, innovative thoughts into your mind, but how to get old ones out."

— Dee Hock, Founder of Visa

"The things we fear most in organizations –
fluctuations, disturbances, imbalances – are the
primary sources of creativity."

— Margaret J. Wheatley, Management Consultant

"The greatest barrier to success is the fear of failure."

— Sven Goran Eriksson, Famous Football Manager

"The customer is a rear-view mirror, not a guide to the future."

— George Colony, Forrester Research

"Out there in some garage is an entrepreneur who's forging a bullet with your company's name on it."

—Gary Hamel, Business Writer

"Confidence is contagious; so is lack of confidence."

—Vince Lombardi

"The best way to predict the future is to invent it."

—Alan Kay, father of the personal computer

"Sometimes when you innovate, you make mistakes. It is best to admit them quickly and get on with improving your other innovations."

— Steve Jobs

"Winning is not a sometime thing; it's an all time thing. You don't win once in a while, you don't do things right once in a while, you do them right all the time. Winning is habit. Unfortunately, so is losing."

— Vince Lombardi

"Never interrupt your enemy when he is making a mistake."

— Napoleon Bonaparte

"People rarely buy what they need. They buy what they want."

—Seth Godin – American author, entrepreneur, marketer, and public speaker

"Stay self-funded as long as possible."

— Garrett Camp, founder of Expa, Uber and StumbleUpon

"You only have to do a very few things right in your life so long as you don't do too many things wrong."

— Warren Buffett

"To succeed in business, to reach the top, an individual must know all it is possible to know about that business."

— J. Paul Getty – American industrialist

"You do not lead by hitting people over the head –
that's assault, not leadership."

— Dwight D. Eisenhower

"When cost is number one in importance, you've already lost."

— Jim Rembach, Six Sigma Consultant

"Your income is directly related to your philosophy, NOT the economy."

— Jim Rohn – American entrepreneur, author and motivational speaker

"To be successful, you have to have your heart in your business, and your business in your heart."

— Sr. Thomas Watson

"Success in business requires training and discipline and hard work. But if you're not frightened by these things, the opportunities are just as great today as they ever were."

— David Rockefeller

"Whether you think you can or whether you think you can't, you're right!"

– Henry Ford

"I'm a great believer in luck, and find the harder I work, the more I have of it."

— Thomas Jefferson

"A business has to be involving, it has to be fun, and it has to exercise your creative instincts."

— Richard Branson

"We generate fears while we sit. We overcome them by action. Fear is nature's way of warning us to get busy."

— Dr. Henry Link

"You have brains in your head. You have feet in your shoes. You can steer yourself, any direction you choose."

— Dr. Seuss

"Change is not a threat, it's an opportunity. Survival is not the goal, transformative success is."

— Seth Godin

"Business is more exciting than any game."

— Lord Beaverbrook

"People don't take opportunities because the timing is bad, the financial side unsecure. Too many people are overanalyzing. Sometimes you just have to go for it."

— Michelle Zatly, Co-founder of SoundFlare

"Surviving a failure gives you more self–confidence. Failures are great learning tools... but they must be kept to a minimum."

— Jeffrey Immelt

"Yesterday's home runs don't win today's games."

— Babe Ruth

"Don't take too much advice. Most people who have a lot of advice to give — with a few exceptions — generalize whatever they did. Don't over-analyze everything. I myself have been guilty of over-thinking problems. Just build things and find out if they work."

— Ben Silbermann, Pinterest founder

"I like thinking big. If you're going to be thinking anything, you might as well think big."

— Donald Trump

"No one is born a CEO, but no one tells you that. The magazine stories make it sound like Mark Zuckerberg woke up one day and wanted to redefine how the world communicates [by creating] a billion-dollar company. He didn't."

— Andrew W. "Drew" Houston, founder and CEO of Dropbox

"When you innovate, you've got to be prepared for everyone telling you you're nuts."

— Larry Ellison

"The successful man is the one who finds out what is the matter with his business before his competitors do."

— Roy L. Smith

"I can accept failure, everyone fails at something. But I can't accept not trying."

— Michael Jordan

"Please think about your legacy, because you're writing it every day."

— Gary Vaynerchuck

"The man who will use his skill and constructive imagination to see how much he can give for a dollar, instead of how little he can give for a dollar, is bound to succeed."

— Henry Ford

"Luck is a dividend of sweat. The more you sweat, the luckier you get."

— Ray Kroc, McDonald's founder

"The new source of power is not money in the hands of a few, but information in the hands of many."

— John Naisbitt

"Business in a combination of war and sport."

— Andre Maurois

"A man who wants to lead the orchestra must turn his back on the crowd."

— Max Lucado

"To the degree we're not living our dreams; our comfort zone has more control of us than we have over ourselves."

— Peter McWilliams

"I don't think an economic slump will hurt good ideas."

— Rob Kalin, Etsy founder

"I have not failed. I've just found 10,000 ways that won't work."

— Thomas Edison

"The critical ingredient is getting off your butt and doing something. It's as simple as that. A lot of people have ideas, but there are few who decide to do something about them now. Not tomorrow. Not next week. But today. The true entrepreneur is a doer, not a dreamer."

— Nolan Bushnell

"Trust your instincts."

— Estee Lauder, Estee Lauder founder

"The golden rule for every business man is this: Put yourself in your customer's place."

— Orison Swett Marden

"If you just work on stuff that you like and you're passionate about, you don't have to have a master plan with how things will play out."

— Mark Zuckerberg, Facebook founder

"It is not the strongest of the species that survive, nor the most intelligent, but the one most responsive to change."

— Charles Darwin

"If you can't fly then run, if you can't run then walk,
if you can't walk then crawl, but whatever you do,
you have to keep moving forward."

— Martin Luther King, Jr.

"To win without risk is to triumph without glory."

— Pierre Corneille

"I don't pay good wages because I have a lot of money; I have a lot of money because I pay good wages."

— Robert Bosch

"Paying attention to simple little things that most men neglect makes a few men rich."

— Henry Ford

"To succeed... You need to find something to hold on to, something to motivate you, something to inspire you."

— Tony Dorsett

"Embrace what you don't know, especially in the beginning, because what you don't know can become your greatest asset. It ensures that you will absolutely be doing things different from everybody else."

— Sara Blakely, SPANX founder

"Any business plan won't survive its first encounter with reality. The reality will always be different. It will never be the plan."

— Jeff Bezos, founder and CEO of Amazon.com

"Early to bed and early to rise probably indicates unskilled labor."

— John Ciardi

"If you really want the key to success, start by doing the opposite of what everyone else is doing."

— Brad Szollose

"Opportunity is missed by most people because it is dressed in overalls and looks like work."

— Thomas Edison

"Those who are blessed with the most talent don't necessarily outperform everyone else. It's the people with follow-through who excel."

— Mary Kay Ash

"Fail often so you can succeed sooner."

— Tom Kelley, Ideo partner

"People are best convinced by things they themselves discover."

— Ben Franklin

"Statistics suggest that when customers complain, business owners and managers ought to get excited about it. The complaining customer represents a huge opportunity for more business."

— Zig Ziglar

"See things in the present, even if they are in the future."

— Larry Ellison, Oracle co-founder

"If it really was a no–brainer to make it on your own in business there'd be millions of no–brained, harebrained, and otherwise dubiously brained individuals quitting their day jobs and hanging out their own shingles. Nobody would be left to round out the workforce and execute the business plan."

— Bill Rancic

"A successful man is one who can lay a firm foundation with the bricks others have thrown at him."

— David Brinkley

"In the business world, everyone is paid in two coins: cash and experience. Take the experience first; the cash will come later."

— Harold Geneen

"Successful people are the ones who are breaking the rules."

— Seth Godin

"Walt Disney told his crew to 'build the castle first' when constructing Disney World, knowing that vision would continue to serve as motivation throughout the project. Oftentimes when people fail to achieve what they want in life, it's because their vision isn't strong enough."

— Gail Blanke, President and CEO, Lifedesigns

"You have to be burning with an idea, or a problem, or a wrong that you want to right. If you're not passionate enough from the start, you'll never stick it out."

— Steve Jobs

"There is no security on the earth, there is only opportunity."

— General Douglas MacArthur

"The important thing is not being afraid to take a chance. Remember, the greatest failure is to not try. Once you find something you love to do, be the best at doing it."

— Debbi Fields

"A person who is quietly confident makes the best leader."

— Fred Wilson, Union Square Ventures co-founder

"Long–range planning works best in the short term."

— Doug Evelyn

"Chase the vision, not the money, the money will end up following you."

— Tony Hsieh, Zappos C

"Get five or six of your smartest friends in a room
and ask them to rate your idea."

— Mark Pincus, Zynga CEO

"To think is easy. To act is difficult. To act as one thinks is the most difficult."

— Johann Wolfgang Von Goeth

"You don't learn to walk by following rules. You learn by doing and falling over."

— Sir Richard Branson, Virgin Group founder

"Your most unhappy customers are your greatest source of learning."

— Bill Gates

"If you work just for money, you'll never make it, but if you love what you're doing and you always put the customer first, success will be yours."

— Ray Kroc, McDonald's founder

"Never put off till tomorrow what you can do today."

— Thomas Jefferson

"The greatest leader is not necessarily the one who does the greatest things. He is the one that gets the people to do the greatest things."

— Ronald Reagan

"Winners take time to relish their work, knowing that scaling the mountain is what makes the view from the top so exhilarating."

— Denis Waitley

"Never tell someone how to do something. Just tell them what needs to be done and they will amaze you with their ingenuity."

— General George S. Patton

"Winning is a habit. Unfortunately so is losing"

— Vincent Lombardi

"Get big quietly, so you don't tip off potential competitors."

— Chris Dixon, Andreesen Horowitz investor

"You don't need to have a 100-person company to develop that idea."

— Larry Page, Google co-founder

"Being defeated is often a temporary condition. Giving up is what makes it permanent."

— Marilyn vos Savant

"Are you a serial idea–starting person? The goal is to be an idea–shipping person."

— Seth Godin

"It's not that we need new ideas, but we need to stop having old ideas."

— Edwin Land, Polaroid co-founder

"When I dare to be powerful, to use my strength in the service of my vision, then it becomes less and less important whether I am afraid."

— Audre Lorde

"Whatever the mind of man can conceive and believe, it can achieve. Thoughts are things! And powerful things at that, when mixed with definiteness of purpose, and burning desire, can be translated into riches."

— Napoleon Hill

"Make every detail perfect and limit the number of details to perfect."

— Jack Dorsey, Twitter co-founder

"Don't play games that you don't understand, even if you see lots of other people making money from them."

— Tony Hsieh, Zappos CEO

"When you delve deep enough, you find that practically every great fortune and great enterprise in America has sprung from the courage enterprise of some individuals. It was Commodore Vanderbilt's enterprise in switching first from running a ferryboat to running other ships, and then, when he was well along in years, his enterprise in switching into railroading that created what was to become one of the most notable fortunes in the history of the world."

— B.C. Forbes, journalist and founder of Forbes magazine

"It's kind of fun to do the impossible."

— Walt Disney

"Entrepreneur is someone who has a vision for something and a want to create."

— David Karp, Tumblr founder and CEO

"Risk more than others think is safe. Dream more than others think is practical."

— Howard Schultz, Starbucks CEO

"Fortunes are built during the down market and collected in the up market."

— Jason Calacanis, LAUNCH Ticker founder

"What do you need to start a business? Three simple things: know your product better than anyone. Know your customer, and have a burning desire to succeed."

— Dave Thomas, Founder, Wendy's

"Your work is going to fill a large part of your life, and the only way to be truly satisfied is to do what you believe is great work. And the only way to do great work is to love what you do."

— Steve Jobs, Apple Inc. co-founder, chairman and CEO

"Genius is one percent inspiration and ninety–nine percent perspiration"

— Thomas A. Edison

"Always deliver more than expected."

— Larry Page, Google co-founder

"The secret to successful hiring is this: look for the people who want to change the world."

— Marc Benioff, Salesforce CEO

"You jump off a cliff and you assemble an airplane on the way down."

— Reid Hoffman, LinkedIn co-founder

"You shouldn't focus on why you can't do something, which is what most people do. You should focus on why perhaps you can, and be one of the exceptions."

— Steve Case, AOL co-founder

"What do you need to start a business? Three simple things: know your product better than anyone. Know your customer, and have a burning desire to succeed."

— Dave Thomas, Wendy's founder

"I knew that if I failed I wouldn't regret that, but I knew the one thing I might regret is not trying."

— Jeff Bezos, Amazon founder and CEO

"I never took a day off in my twenties. Not one."

— Bill Gates, Microsoft co-founder

"The most dangerous poison is the feeling of achievement. The antidote is to every evening think what can be done better tomorrow."

— Ingvar Kamprad, IKEA founder

"Don't be afraid to assert yourself, have confidence in your abilities and don't let the bastards get you down."

— Michael Bloomberg, Bloomberg L.P. founder

"Whenever you see a successful business, someone once made a courageous decision."

— Peter F. Drucker

"If you're going to put your product in beta – put your business model in beta with it."

— Joe Kraus, Google Ventures partner

"There is a difference between being a leader and being a boss. Both are based on authority. A boss demands blind obedience; a leader earns his authority through understanding and trust."

— Klaus Balkenhol

"Data beats emotions."

— Sean Rad, Adly and Tinder founder

"I like to pride myself on thinking pretty long term,
but not that long term."

— Mark Zuckerberg, Facebook founder

"Theory is splendid but until put into practice, it is valueless."

— James Cash Penney, J.C. Penney founder

"The fastest way to change yourself is to hang out with people who are already the way you want to be."

— Reid Hoffman, LinkedIn co-founder

"When you find an idea that you just can't stop thinking about, that's probably a good one to pursue."

— Josh James, Omniture CEO and co-founder

"I made a resolve then that I was going to amount to something if I could. And no hours, nor amount of labor, nor amount of money would deter me from giving the best that there was in me. And I have done that ever since, and I win by it. I know."

— Harland Sanders, KFC founder

"In the end, a vision without the ability to execute it is probably a hallucination."

— Steve Case, AOL co-founder

"No guts, no story."

— Chris Brady

"We are really competing against ourselves, we have no control over how other people perform."

— Pete Cashmore, Mashable founder and CEO

"You just have to pay attention to what people need and what has not been done."

— Russell Simmons, Def Jam founder

"Expect the unexpected, and whenever possible, be the unexpected."

— Lynda Berry

"A business that makes nothing but money is a poor business."

— Henry Ford, founder of Ford Motor Company

"The way to get started is to quit talking and begin doing."

— Walt Disney, Disney founder

"Always bear in mind that your own resolution to succeed is more important than any other one thing."

— Abraham Lincoln

"Sometimes by losing a battle you find a new way to win the war."

— Donald Trump

"Don't worry about failure; you only have to be right once."

— Drew Houston, Dropbox founder and CEO

"If you're passionate about something and you work hard, then I think you will be successful."

— Pierre Omidyar, Ebay founder and chairman

"Business has only two functions – marketing and innovation."

— Peter Drucker

"You gain strength, courage and confidence by every experience in which you really stop to look fear in the face. You are able to say to yourself, "I lived through this horror. I can take the next thing that comes along." You must do the thing you think you cannot do."

— Eleanor Roosevelt

"Your time is limited, so don't waste it living someone else's life."

— Steve Jobs

"If you spend your life trying to be good at everything, you will never be great at anything."

— Tom Rath

"If you're not a risk taker, you should get the hell out of business."

— Ray Kroc, McDonald's founder

"Stay self-funded as long as possible."

— Garrett Camp, Canadian entrepreneur who co-founded StumbleUpon and Uber.

"There is no royal flower-strewn path to success. And if there is, I have not found it, for if I have accomplished anything in life it is because I have been willing to work hard."

— Madam C.J. Walker, America's first female entrepreneur millionaire

"To succeed in business, to reach the top, an individual must know all it is possible to know about that business."

— J. Paul Getty

"In a battle between two ideas, the best one doesn't necessarily win. No, the idea that wins is the one with the most fearless heretic behind it."

— Seth Godin

"So often people are working hard at the wrong thing. Working on the right thing is probably more important than working hard."

— Caterina Fake, Co-founder, Flickr

"A good plan violently executed now is better than a
perfect plan executed next week."

— George Patton

"All our dreams can come true – if we have the courage to pursue them."

— Walt Disney

"My interest in life comes from setting myself huge, apparently unachievable challenges and trying to rise above them."

— Richard Branson

"Management is doing things right; leadership is doing the right things."

— Peter F. Drucker

"My job is not to be easy on people. My job is to take these great people we have and to push them and make them even better."

— Steve Jobs

"Success is a lousy teacher. It seduces smart people into thinking they can't lose."

— Bill Gates

"You don't learn to walk by following rules. You learn by doing and falling over."

— Richard Branson, Virgin Group founder

"In the end, it is important to remember that we cannot become what we need to be by remaining what we are."

— Max De Pree

Conclusion

Thank you again for buying this book!

I hope this book was able to help you with your motivation and inspiration, which are both so important in business and life. Read these famous quotes often, and also whenever you feel down, whenever you feel that things are not going your way, and you will surely bounce back. Share these quotes with your friends and co-workers too, because everyone faces down-time and challenges in life and work. I am sure that they are going to find these quotes most useful too.

Remember, everyone faces problems. No, you are not alone. It's the ability to keep doing what you are best at, through difficult times that make the critical difference between eventual success and failure. Nothing is over till you are completely done. You have the ability to bounce back always, even if it feels like an impossible task.

So do read these inspirational quotes often, whenever you feel like. I am sure that they are going to help you a great deal.

Thank you and good luck!

Paul White

Printed in Great Britain
by Amazon